12 SCARY
ANIMALS

by Allan Morey

12 STORY LIBRARY

www.12StoryLibrary.com

12-Story Library is an imprint of Peterson Publishing Company and Press Room Editions.

Produced for 12-Story Library by Red Line Editorial

Photographs ©: Markuso/Shutterstock Images, cover, 1; Serge_Vero/iStockphoto, 4; François Louis Nompar de Caumont LaPorte, 5; Nomis Simon CC2.0, 6, 29; dennisvdw/iStockphoto, 7; Nippel/Shutterstock Images, 8; Stacey Newman/iStockphoto, 9; Anette Andersen/iStockphoto, 10; NOAA NMFS Santa Cruz Laboratory Library, 11; B. G. Wilder, 12; David Starr Jordan/Freshwater and Marine Image Bank/University of Washington, 13; Patrick K. Campbell/Shutterstock Images, 14; David Persson/Shutterstock Images, 15; kurt_G/Shutterstock Images, 16, 28; Calvin Ang/Shutterstock Images, 17; contrail1/iStockphoto, 19; Sergey Uryadnikov/Shutterstock Images, 20; Ethan Daniels/Shutterstock Images, 21; Olgysha/Shutterstock Images, 22; Khoroshunova Olga/Shutterstock Images, 23; Matt Jeppson/Shutterstock Images, 24; Derek L Miller/Shutterstock Images, 25; Dennis Donohue/iStockphoto/Thinkstock, 26; Pablo Jacinto Yoder/Shutterstock Images, 27

Library of Congress Cataloging-in-Publication Data
Names: Morey, Allan, author.
Title: 12 scary animals / by Allan Morey.
Other titles: Twelve scary animals
Description: North Mankato, MN : 12-Story Library, [2017] | Series: Scary and
    spooky | Audience: Grades 4 to 6. | Includes bibliographical references
    and index.
Identifiers: LCCN 2016002353 (print) | LCCN 2016007045 (ebook) | ISBN
    9781632352958 (library bound : alk. paper) | ISBN 9781632353450 (pbk. :
    alk. paper) | ISBN 9781621434610 (hosted ebook)
Subjects: LCSH: Dangerous animals--Miscellanea--Juvenile literature. |
    Animals--Miscellanea--Juvenile literature.
Classification: LCC QL100 .M67 2017 (print) | LCC QL100 (ebook) | DDC
    591.6/5--dc23
LC record available at http://lccn.loc.gov/2016002353

Printed in the United States of America
Mankato, MN
May, 2016

Access free, up-to-date content on this topic plus a full digital version of this book. Scan the QR code on page 31 or use your school's login at 12StoryLibrary.com.

Table of Contents

Amazonian Giant Centipedes Stalk in the Night

In the rain forest, the scariest animals come out at night. Dark wings swoop through the air. Eyes glow green in the moonlight. And creatures skitter across the jungle floor. These animals are hunting for food. Among them is the Amazonian giant centipede.

This centipede is a monster among its kind. It can grow more than 12 inches (30 cm) long. That is about the size of a person's forearm. The centipede's body is armor plated. Each of its many legs ends in a pointy claw. These claws are perfect for holding prey or climbing up trees and cave

walls. The centipedes are super fast thanks to all those legs.

Similar to other centipedes, the Amazonian giant has a venomous bite. It injects poison into its prey with two sharp pincers near its mouth.

The Amazonian giant centipede is one of the largest centipede species.

The venom is painful to people. It is deadly to small animals. Amazonian giant centipedes eat rodents, frogs, lizards, and spiders.

These centipedes also eat bats. They climb to the ceilings of caves. Then they hang upside down. They cannot see very well. But their antennae sense movement. They know when a bat flies nearby. The centipedes snag bats out of midair. They deliver a quick, deadly dose of venom. Then they begin to eat their meal.

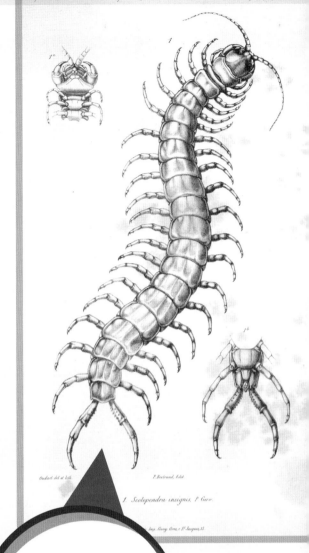

This drawing shows close-up sketches of the Amazonian giant centipede.

46
Number of legs Amazonian giant centipedes have.

- Amazonian giant centipedes have claws on the tips of their legs for grasping prey.
- They are great climbers and can chase prey up into trees.
- Even in the dark, these centipedes can locate prey with their antennae.
- They have a venomous bite.

Aye-ayes Haunt the Rain Forests

Not all scary animals have razor-sharp claws or venom-filled fangs. Some are terrifying because of the way they look. This is true of aye-ayes. They look the same as mini-monsters in a scary movie.

Aye-ayes are a type of primate. They have grasping hands and feet similar to monkeys and apes. They live in the rain forests of Madagascar. This island is off the coast of Africa. Aye-ayes are good at climbing. They spend their lives in the treetops.

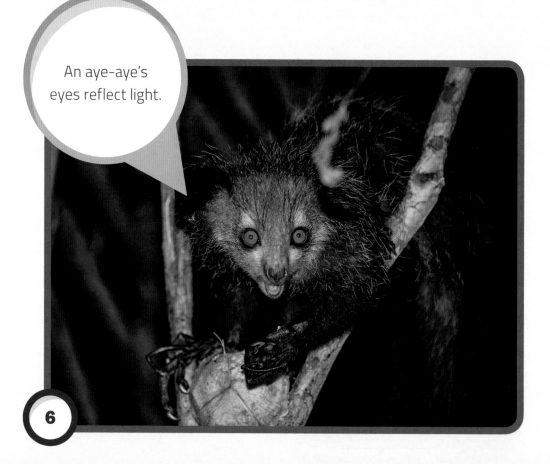

An aye-aye's eyes reflect light.

They eat fruit from the trees and hunt for bugs.

Aye-ayes are believed to be the only primate that uses echolocation to find food. They tap on tree bark with their long fingers. Then they listen to the echo of their tapping. The sound tells them where bugs are under the bark.

Aye-ayes are too small to harm people. But they still frighten the people who live on Madagascar. Aye-ayes are nocturnal. They have excellent night vision. Glowing eyes in the treetops can be scary. This creepy factor has led some people to believe that aye-ayes are evil. The people of Madagascar think aye-ayes bring bad luck. These furry critters are often killed. They are now in danger of extinction.

The aye-aye is an endangered animal.

THINK ABOUT IT

Every culture believes certain things bring bad luck. The people of Madagascar think this about aye-ayes. What unique beliefs do people have about an animal that lives near you? Where do these beliefs come from?

2
Number of types of primates.

- Aye-ayes are a type of primate with grasping hands and feet.
- They live in the rain forests of Madagascar.
- Aye-ayes use echolocation to find food.
- They have excellent night vision.

Shocking Electric Eels

Many deadly critters live in the waters of the Amazon River. One of these animals is the electric eel. Electric eels were misnamed. They are not eels. Eels are snakelike fish without any shocking power. Electric eels are closer to knife fish. These are fish that have the ability to create bursts of electricity. Knife fish also have long bodies and a fin running along their bellies.

The "electric" part of the eels' name is fitting. It is what makes them scary. Their bursts of electricity are about five times as powerful as a standard house outlet.

Electric eels use their shocking power to hunt and protect themselves.

Unlike most fish, electric eels must go to the water's surface often to breathe.

ELECTRICITY

All animals generate some electricity. The cells in their muscles create tiny electrical charges as they move. In most animals, the charges are too small to feel. Electric eels have thousands of specialized muscle cells. They are lined up along their bodies similar to a row of batteries in a flashlight. The muscles create an electrical circuit with shocking results.

The shocking power helps electric eels catch prey. It is hard to see in the murky waters of the Amazon. Electric eels also have poor eyesight. Their electric power guides them. They send out small bursts of electricity to help them find prey. Once they sense that food is near, they give off a large burst of electricity. This stuns everything in the water around them. Then the eel eats the stunned animals. This might include fish, frogs, small birds, and mammals. The power of an electric eel is not deadly to people. But it can still stun a person.

600
Number of volts an electric eel can generate in one shock.

- Electric eels live in the waters of the Amazon River.
- They can create small bursts of energy.
- Electric eels' shocking power helps them find food.
- They stun everything in the water around them and then eat the stunned animals.

Fangtooths Lurk in Ocean Depths

Most of the Earth is covered in water. Some of the world's oceans extend miles deep. Scientists have not been able to thoroughly explore the deepest parts because of the crushing pressure. But some of the creatures from the ocean's depths are beyond scary. One of these animals is the fangtooth.

Little light shines where the fangtooth lives. The fangtooth has poor eyesight. But that

> Scientists have learned a lot about fangtooths by studying fossils.

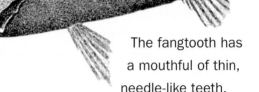

Fangtooths have large, sharp teeth.

The fangtooth has a mouthful of thin, needle-like teeth. Its front fangs are very long. It looks as if the fangtooth could not close its mouth. But it has holes in its jaw into which the long front teeth slide.

does not keep it from finding food. Swimming around in the dark means it runs into things. Scientists think fangtooth can sense chemicals given off by other animals. This ability quickly lets the fangtooth know if it has bumped into food or not. If it meets a small fish or squid, the fangtooth eats it.

ANGLERFISH

Anglerfish are another type of scary-looking, deep-sea fish. They have a unique way of attracting prey. A growth sticks out of the female anglerfish's forehead. At the end of it is a bulb of flesh that glows. The light attracts other animals. Then the anglerfish gobbles them up.

16,500
Depth, in feet (5,000 m), where fangtooths have been found.

- Fangtooths live deeper in the ocean than many other fish.
- They have poor eyesight so they often run into things.
- Fangtooths can sense chemicals given off by other animals.
- They have long, needle-like teeth, which are perfect for snatching food.

11

5

Ghastly Looking Goblin Sharks

Goblin sharks live in the dark depths of the ocean. They are scary because of their size. They have rows of interlocking, needle-like teeth. These teeth curve inward to help goblin sharks hold onto their food.

Goblin sharks are rarely seen. They have been found at more than 4,000 feet (1,219 m) deep.

Normally they live in water that is between 885 and 3,100 feet (270 and 940 m) deep. But sometimes they swim into shallower waters to feed. When they do, they can get caught in deep-sea fishing nets. Goblin sharks have been caught in the Gulf of Mexico and near Japan and Australia.

Goblin sharks are similar to other sharks, except for one feature. Their jaws are held back beneath their snouts. But when feeding, their jaws shoot out to snatch at prey. With their jaws jutting forward, they

Goblin sharks are sometimes called living fossils.

Fig. 133 —Goblin- hark (Tenguzame), *Mitsukurina owstoni* Jordan. Fr...... Imperial University of Tokyo.

look similar to a monster from the movies. They mostly feed on fish, squid, shrimp, and octopuses.

Goblin sharks have rounded fins, rather than pointed ones.

FEELING ELECTRIC

All sharks have a sixth sense. Near their snouts are sensors that detect small amounts of electricity. This is the energy that animals give off when they move their muscles. Even in dark, murky water, sharks can find their prey. With their wide heads, hammerhead sharks have more sensors than any other shark. They can even locate stingrays buried in the sand.

13

Length, in feet (4 m), of the largest goblin shark.

- Goblin sharks have rows of interlocking teeth.
- They are rarely seen because they live in deep waters.
- Some goblin sharks have gotten caught in fishing nets.
- Their jaws shoot out to catch prey.

13

6

Green Anacondas Are the Heavyweights of Snakes

There is debate about which snake is the largest in the world. If judged by weight, green anacondas win. Green anacondas live in the Amazon rain forest. They prefer to prowl in the water. The water makes it easier for these snakes to move their heavy bodies. It is also a good place to wait for their next meal.

When an animal bends down for a drink, the anaconda strikes. It does not have sharp fangs as other venomous snakes do. Instead, it has small, pointed teeth that curve inward. They are perfect for grasping and holding onto prey. The anaconda wraps its muscular body around the

Green anacondas are mostly green in color, but also have black spots on their bodies.

Green anacondas can move faster in water than on land.

prey once it is caught. The anaconda squeezes as the animal breathes out. This prevents it from being able to breathe in. Eventually the prey chokes from the bone-crushing pressure of the anaconda squeezing it. Anacondas eat deer, pigs, rodents, and birds. They even tangle with caimans and eat these alligator-like reptiles.

500

Weight, in pounds (227 kg), of the largest green anaconda.

- Green anacondas are the largest snakes in the world based on weight.
- They wait for their food in the water.
- Green anacondas strike with their small, pointed teeth.
- They squeeze the animal until it cannot breathe any longer.

THINK ABOUT IT

Review the facts about anacondas on these pages. What features make this snake scary? Why do you think the author included it on a list of 12 scary animals? Can you think of other scary animals that hunt their prey?

15

Huntsman Spiders Are the Size of Dinner Plates

Many people find spiders terrifying. They are creepy and crawly. And most have venomous bites. Imagine a spider the size of a dinner plate! That is how big the giant huntsman spider can grow.

There are thousands of species of huntsman spiders. They are found in tropical areas around the world. But the largest among them is the giant huntsman. It lives in Southeast Asia.

GOLIATH BIRD-EATING SPIDERS

The Goliath bird-eating spider is a type of tarantula. It is one of the largest spiders. It grows nearly 12 inches (30 cm) long and has 1-inch (2.5-cm) fangs. Goliath bird-eating spiders are thicker and outweigh giant huntsman spiders. But the Goliath is much slower than the speedy huntsman.

This spider's body is about the size of a person's palm. They have long legs. They can run sideways as well as dart forward.

Huntsman spiders do not build webs or wait for

Huntsman spiders have eight eyes.

Huntsman spiders eat small insects.

a meal to fly nearby. They hunt for their food. Giant huntsman spiders eat insects and small rodents.

These spiders have fangs. They inject venom into their prey through the fangs. This poison is deadly to the spider's prey. It is not deadly, only painful, for humans.

The giant huntsman is sometimes confused with a tarantula. But the two types of spiders are easy to tell apart by their legs. Tarantulas bend their legs under their bodies. Huntsman spiders spread their legs out.

12
Length, in inches (30 cm), of a huntsman spider's leg span.

- Huntsman spiders are the size of a dinner plate.
- They do not build webs and wait for food.
- Instead, huntsman spiders hunt for their prey.
- They can inject venom into their prey through their fangs.

Japanese Giant Hornets Attack Their Targets

People avoid being stung by hornets and wasps. But imagine what would happen if they saw a hornet the size of their thumb! Japanese giant hornets are the world's largest hornets.

As their name hints, Japanese giant hornets live in Japan. They are related to the giant Asian hornets found in eastern Asia. But giant hornets are beginning to move around the world. Sometimes they get stuck in cargo shipments going to Europe and the Americas. The insects make homes in these new areas.

Japanese giant hornets are mean predators. A nest sends out a few scouts to look for beehives of other hornet species. Once they find one, they show the rest of their nest

THINK ABOUT IT

An invasive animal species is one that is introduced to an area where it does not naturally live. What negative effects might invasive species, such as Japanese giant hornets, cause in an area that is not its natural home?

2.5

Length, in inches (6.4 cm), of a Japanese giant hornet's wingspan.

- Japanese giant hornets are the world's largest hornets.
- They live in Japan but are starting to be seen elsewhere.
- Giant hornets send out scouts to find food and then swarm.
- They have painful and sometimes deadly stings.

Japanese giant hornets can grow almost 2 inches (5.1 cm) long.

where to find food. Then the giant hornets attack. Their large jaws easily cut insects in half. And a couple of dozen Japanese giant hornets can destroy a beehive that has tens of thousands of bees. The giant hornets carry the remains of the dead bees back to their nest after the attack. The dead bees become food for the giant hornets' young.

Japanese giant hornets are extremely aggressive. They will swarm and attack anyone who comes too close or disturbs their nests. Their stings are painful and filled with venom. Many deaths from giant hornet stings are reported each year in Japan.

Venomous Komodo Dragons Stalk Their Prey

Have you ever seen a lizard in your backyard? It probably was not scary. But imagine if it was 10 feet (3 m) long. That would be frightening! Komodo dragons are the world's largest lizards. They are also the world's largest venomous animals. These beasts are found on a few small islands in the country of Indonesia. They got their name for being found on Komodo Island. They live mostly in hot, dry forests and grasslands.

Komodo dragon venom will not kill an animal quickly. But it still can be deadly. Komodo dragons sneak up on their prey. This includes deer, wild pigs, or even water buffalo. Then in a quick burst of speed, the Komodo dragon darts in for a nip with its razor-sharp teeth. Often their prey gets away after the first bite.

A Komodo dragon follows its prey after it has been bitten. Other Komodo dragons pick up the smell

Komodo dragons can live up to 30 years.

300

Weight, in pounds (136 kg), of a Komodo dragon.

- Komodo dragons are the world's largest lizards.
- They live on a few small islands in Indonesia.
- Their venom can be deadly and kills slowly.
- Komodo dragons kill their prey when it has become weak.

VENOMOUS LIZARDS

Until a few years ago, scientists thought there were only two species of venomous lizards: Gila monsters and Mexican bearded lizards. Both are found in North America. But recently, scientists have discovered they were wrong. Many more lizards are venomous than they thought. These lizards include members of the monitor lizard and iguana families.

from the wound. They also begin to follow the animal. Meanwhile, the Komodo dragon's venom slowly weakens the injured animal.

It could take days or weeks for the injured animal to die. Komodo dragons are patient. They follow the injured creature until the venom makes their prey too weak to defend itself. Then they go in for the kill.

Komodo dragons are protected in Indonesia.

Mantis Shrimp Are the Ocean's Punching Champs

Size does not always matter when it comes to deadly strength. That is true of the mantis shrimp. Some of these critters grow only a few inches long. But their punches can break bones and shatter shells.

Mantis shrimp are built to hunt. They have excellent eyesight. They can see many more colors than other animals. They can even see colors that people cannot. Mantis shrimp's eyes are on stalks. They can move them independently from each other. This helps them to see all around. It also makes it difficult for prey to hide from them.

Mantis shrimp are a variety of colors including shades of brown and brighter colors.

Mantis shrimp hide in holes and burrows.

Mantis shrimp are fast. They scurry along the ocean floor on their many pairs of legs. If they need an extra burst of speed while chasing prey, they flick their tails.

Mantis shrimp are believed to have the most powerful strike of any animal. They have claws that they use like how a fist is used. The mantis can move these claws faster than the blink of an eye. The force they create is enough to crack open the shell of an animal on which a mantis shrimp wants to feed. Mantis shrimp eat crabs, oysters, snails, and many other small critters.

2
Number of claws a mantis shrimp has.

- Some mantis shrimp are only a few inches long.
- They have excellent eyesight and can see many colors.
- Their eyes move independently from each other.
- Mantis shrimp use their claws to punch their prey.

Short-horned Lizards Spray Blood

Some animals scare people because they are big and strong. Or they are fast and deadly. Yet others are scary because of something weird they do. That is true of short-horned lizards. These animals squirt blood out of their eyes!

Short-horned lizards are scaly, spiky reptiles. They got their name because of the horn-like spikes atop their heads. These lizards can be yellow, gray, or reddish-brown. They live in deserts in the western United States. They can also be found in dry areas stretching down through Mexico.

Short-horned lizards are not big. They are usually less than 6 inches (15 cm) long. Snakes, coyotes, and

When short-horned lizards are threatened, their coloring becomes more intense.

hawks prey on them. But these lizards have a few ways to scare off predators. First, they puff up their bodies. This helps them look similar to a spiked ball. One of these lizards might be too much of a mouthful for some animals, especially a snake that swallows its food whole.

If puffing up and looking bigger does not frighten predators, then short-horned lizards have another trick. This trick confuses many animals. Short-horned lizards can squirt blood from their eye ducts. The blood smells and tastes bad. This drives many predators away.

3

Distance, in feet (1 m), that the blood from a short-horned lizard's eyes can shoot.

- Short-horned lizards' bodies are covered in spikes.
- Their coloring is similar to their desert surroundings.
- They can puff up their bodies to make themselves look bigger.
- They squirt blood from ducts near their eyes to confuse predators.

These lizards have a wide range of habitats.

Vampire Bats Are Real-Life Blood Suckers

Rumors of bloodthirsty vampires have scared people for ages. Many stories are simply old legends. But real bloodsuckers can be found in Central and South America.

Vampire bats are named after vampires, and for a good reason. These bats live on the blood of other animals. Livestock, such as cattle and horses, are their usual prey. But they have also been known to feed on people.

Vampire bats do not kill their victims. Usually the bats sneak up on sleeping prey. Then they nip the animals with their sharp, pointy fangs. Instead of sucking the blood, they lap it up from the wound. A

Vampire bats live in groups in dark areas such as caves.

substance in their saliva keeps the blood flowing.

To get food without waking their prey, vampire bats need to be very sneaky. They have the ability to hop or crawl. Their strong hind legs also help them leap into the air to take off. They are usually able to feed off their victims without the animals ever waking.

Vampire bats are most active at night.

9
Average life span of a vampire bat in the wild.

- Vampire bats live in Central and South America.
- They live off the blood of other animals.
- Vampire bats nip their prey with their fangs, then lap up the blood.
- They can hop or crawl.

PARASITES

Parasites are animals that need another animal to survive. Fleas and lice are common parasites. They feed on the blood of their hosts. Some people might consider vampire bats parasites. But unlike other parasites, they do not need to live on a host to survive. The term for this is micropredator. It is a critter that feeds on other animals, but does not need it to survive.

Fact Sheet

- Some animals in this book are at risk of extinction. There are several different endangered statuses. Least concern means there is no threat of extinction. An animal might be in danger of future extinction if they are near threatened. The vulnerable status means an animal is at risk of future extinction. An endangered animal has a high risk of near future extinction. Animals that are critically endangered are almost extinct and only a few are left around the world. Animals that are only found in zoos or sanctuaries are categorized as extinct in the wild. Finally, extinct animals no longer exist in the world.

- Vampire bats are listed as being of least concern. Komodo dragons are vulnerable. Aye-ayes have an endangered status.

- Several animals in this book are nocturnal. Why are animals active at night? There are many reasons. That might be when their prey is out. Nighttime is when they have to hunt. It is cooler at night. The animals do not need protection from the hot, glaring sun. For vampire bats, their prey is asleep at night. This helps them sneak up on cows and other animals.

- Spiders catch food in many ways. Some build webs. Bugs fly into their webs and get stuck in the sticky strands. Trap-door spiders ambush prey. They wait for prey to walk near and then attack. Spitting spiders shoot a mixture of venom and silk at prey. This entraps critters. Bolas spiders cover a sticky strand of silk with a substance. They use it to attract moths. Huntsman spiders and tarantulas go hunting for food.

- The animals in this book are predators. They get energy from feeding on other animals. They are usually larger than the animals they hunt. They have keen senses or special abilities to help them find and catch their prey.

Glossary

echolocation
A method some animals use to locate an object by using an emitted sound and the reflection back from it.

extinction
When a plant or animal species has died out.

invasive species
A plant or animal species that tends to spread.

nocturnal
Active at night.

predators
Animals that prey on others for food.

prey
An animal that is hunted or killed by another for food.

primates
A group of mammals that walk upright and have forward-facing eyes, large brains, and grasping hands.

venom
A poisonous chemical injected, or taken into the body, by a bite or sting.

For More Information

Books

de la Bedoyere, Camilla. *Spiders and Scary Creepy Crawlies.* Orlando, FL: Ripley, 2014. Print.

Rake, Matthew. *Creatures of the Deep.* Minneapolis, MN: Hungry Tomato, 2015. Print.

Spilsbury, Louise. *Superstar Reptiles.* New York: PowerKids, 2015. Print.

Stewart, Melissa. *Deadliest Animals.* Washington, DC: National Geographic, 2011. Print.

Visit 12StoryLibrary.com

Scan the code or use your school's login at **12StoryLibrary.com** for recent updates about this topic and a full digital version of this book. Enjoy free access to:

- Digital ebook
- Breaking news updates
- Live content feeds
- Videos, interactive maps, and graphics
- Additional web resources

Note to educators: Visit 12StoryLibrary.com/register to sign up for free premium website access. Enjoy live content plus a full digital version of every 12-Story Library book you own for every student at your school.

Index

About the Author

Allan Morey grew up on a farm in central Wisconsin. His early love of animals and making up stories led him to a career in writing. Some of his favorite things to write about are animals, sports, ghosts, and monsters. He lives in Minnesota with his wife, two children, and pets.

READ MORE FROM 12-STORY LIBRARY

Every 12-Story Library book is available in many formats. For more information, visit 12StoryLibrary.com.